Table of Contents

Introduction   3

Chapter 1
How big is my opportunity in Mexico?..........................12

Chapter 2
What is the history of NAFTA?..21

Chapter 3
Have you Trademarked your brand in Mexico yet?
If not it may be too late?..29

Chapter 4
Are your labels NOM compliant?...................................35

Chapter 5
Do you know the Correct HS Classification of
your Product?..39

Case studies……………………………………………....45

About the author……………………………………..….49

DISCOVER THE SECRET TREASURE MAP TO SELLING YOUR PRODUCTS IN MEXICO

AND STILL BE HOME IN TIME FOR DINNER

This special serial book is Section 1 of 3 sections of the expert business book:

"The 3 Things you absolutely need to do before you start selling in Mexico."

Copyright © 2012 Sandro Piancone

All rights reserved.

ISBN: 978-1481913201
ISB: 1481913204

Introduction

MEET THE MEXPERT

Hi, my name is Sandro Piancone. I am the Chief Mexpert Officer of *Mexico Sales Made Easy*. Yes, "Mexpert" is a real word, or at least it is now. I trademarked it. I am called the Mexpert for a reason. I'm not a Mexpert because I have a degree in selling in Mexico, or have a degree in international business or finance, but because I have made more mistakes than anyone reading this book. I've spent more money making those mistakes, so that you don't have to. I could write a novel just on the mistakes I have made. My team and I will make sure that you and your company do not make the same mistakes that I have made over the last 14 years.

Of course while making mistakes, I also had some home runs and grand slams. Since 1998, I have generated well over 500 million dollars in sales and profits for my clients and partners helping them export their products into Mexico. *That is why I titled my first book, Discover* **The Secret Treasure Map to Selling your Products in Mexico, and Still be Home in Time for Dinner**. *My clients have found their riches in Mexico. Why not you? Read on.....*

Get your monthly Mexpert Report FREE! Go to..... **www.mexicosalesmadeeasy.com**

Who Am I and What are the Opportunities in Mexico?

My bio says that I am a recovering CEO of a publicly traded food distribution company in Mexico. I took an idea and turned it into a company that became the first nationwide distributor of imported products into Mexico, going from 0 to $100 million dollars in annual revenue in just under 3 years. But that is a story for another day and another book. This book focuses on your ideas for selling in Mexico.

I can't remember being as bullish about the opportunities for American companies exporting to Mexico as I am today. It's not just the dynamics of the Mexican economy. With the economy doing poorly in the United States, and the U.S. government printing money like crazy, there's a hidden benefit. This is making the dollar weak, so that your products seem cheap to the rest of the world, including Mexico, where more than 115 million people live.

Many people, particularly politicians, point out the downsides of the free trade zone between the U.S. and Mexico. Politicians often blame any weaknesses in our own economy on the mechanism of the NAFTA agreement. They have come and gone, but NAFTA is still here and, in fact, working tremendously well and doing what Presidents Reagan and Clinton believed it would.

For example, one of Obama's central policies in his 2008 election campaign was taking apart NAFTA: a policy that, thankfully, has quietly disappeared. We can learn from the controversies of the past.

More importantly, let's look at Mexico, and why I believe it is such a great place to do business now.

Over the last 20 years, Mexico has really started to pull its weight in the world. It's now the 12th largest global economy, and is pushing toward a top ten spot. The Mexican economy is now heavily weighted toward the services sector. With strong emphasis being placed on its education system, Mexico is moving toward a society reliant upon banking, finance, insurance, and retail.

This is a great opportunity for American exporters, not just in food and beverages, but also all manner of other goods aimed at a rapidly growing consumer-based Mexican middle class. Mexico is also a young society, and one that is growing at over 1% each year. That's hardly a population explosion, but with the educational aspirations now inherent within the country, as well as the economic growth being seen now and through the future, the number of middle class consumers is likely to grow quite rapidly from the present 50 million or more who are already in this group. And that's a huge potential target market for all U.S. exporters.

Mexico: a Growth Economy

Indeed, as an indication of the potential growth available, you just have to look at the growth of the Mexican economy and its retail sales. Mexico suffered a horrendous collapse of its economy as a result of the global financial crisis. But the country recovered rapidly.

It's a testament to the political stability of the nation, and good economic management, that her recovery has been so fast, and the economy continues to grow much faster than its NAFTA neighbors. The IMF forecasts for growth over the next two or three years put Mexico with some of the fastest growth economies today. And that growth is available right on our doorstep, not across oceans and half way around the world.

I am also a fan of the way that the Mexican government has a real hand in controlling its finances. Its budget deficit and net national debt is much less than the United States, not just in absolute terms, but more importantly in terms of respective GDP. This gives the Mexican government a huge fist to wield against any future economic shocks.

Times are tough in the United States, and it looks like it's going to be tough for a long time. Taxes are rising, and government spending falling as the huge debt is tackled. Mexico doesn't face such problems. And that's good news for employment there. Mexico's unemployment rate is just a shade above 5%, which in turn is good news for retail sales. And that's going to encourage plenty of imports from the United States.

So, all things considered, it's a great time to be doing business in Mexico. And that brings me to talking about how you can get involved if you're not already, and if you are, how you can improve procedures and processes that will get your product across the border and to the point of sale faster and more efficiently.

I've been in business since I was a kid. I've built businesses from nothing and then sold them on as I moved to new challenges. A great part of my career history is grounded in the food and beverage business, and I've founded and grown fast food and traditional restaurant chains, as well as exporting companies. I suppose really that I was always looking for the business that presented me with the greatest satisfaction. And that's what I've found with *Mexico Sales Made Easy*.

Let Me Show You How to Avoid Costly Mistakes Selling in Mexico

It dawned on me that there are a whole lot of businesses making common mistakes, and because of them, they were being held back from making real riches in Mexico. Eventually, when some U.S. businesses did find their products in place and ready to sell in Mexico, margins had been shot to shreds because of the cost of these common mistakes. To me, this was a great waste. So I decided to do something about it, and founded *Mexico Sales Made Easy (MSME)*.

Mistake #1: Don't Jump in Head First

One of the major mistakes that companies wanting to export to Mexico make is to jump in head first, without properly planning their entry into this lucrative market. You would not believe how many companies I meet at trade shows that have spent tens of thousands of dollars to exhibit at the show, but have not thought about trademarking their products, have not done appropriate NOM-51 labeling for food and beverages, and do not even know the HS number of their products. NOM-51 labeling is the official Mexican system for labeling food and beverages, and products cannot be sold in Mexico without adhering to the NOM-51 system. The HS number refers to the globally Harmonized Commodity Description and Coding System developed and maintained by the World Customs Organization, which is also required for sales in Mexico.

These companies rush to set everything up, get orders on board, and then find that those orders can't be filled because they haven't first taken the time to complete the basic requirements of exporting to Mexico. Orders are lost and the business name is trashed before it even started.

That's what this book tackles, and the first thing that **MSME** tackles. We'll talk to you about your business, your goals, and your potential market. Then we'll do the required work of preparation for success. We'll take care of all your paperwork, ensuring your products are correctly classified, registering trademarks to protect your business from copycats, and making sure all your labeling conforms to current regulations.

Too many companies underestimate how difficult this process can be and how long it can take. Because we have so many years of experience behind us, and it's what we do every day of the week, every week of the year, we'll make this first part of the process as painless as possible.

Once these foundations for export have been put in place, you can then begin the real process of selling into Mexico. And this is what you are good at: it's your product and your market. We consider it our duty to help you with this part of your business: after all, you are our client, and your success is our success. We can't become directly involved, but what we can do is give you the resources that you need to kick start your sales. In Section 2 of this book, we'll cover the second stage of exporting to Mexico: selling, finding distributors, how to do tradeshows, giving tips on method of approach, who to approach, how to do trade road shows and more.

Finally, once you have your initial export paperwork in place and you have won your first orders, now it's time for the business of the export itself. And here, we come back into the game, proactively working on your behalf.

After two decades of working with Mexican customs officials, we not only know and understand the rules, regulations, and methods, but we also know many of those officials as if they were our family. We work hand in hand with them to ensure your exports to Mexico flow smoothly.

Logistics are crucial, and therefore, we recommend a world class logistics company, one of our Titanium clients whose warehouses are among the best in the country. They'll ensure your goods move to their final destination as soon as possible, but while they await inspection and paperwork referencing, they'll be guarded by 24 hour video surveillance, dedicated security guards, and the most comprehensive insurance package available.

Straight Talking in a Language You Understand

¿Qué pasó? What will you experience working with **MSME**? Good business, in a language you understand. Many companies falsely believe that the Mexican market is closed to them because they don't speak Spanish.

Our representatives are experts in the importation of goods and services into Mexico. And they are tri-lingual: Spanish and English come naturally to them, as does the third language: importation law and customs jargon. We explain everything you need to know and more in plain English. That means you understand what is required, when and why. There's no ambiguity, no talking at cross purposes, and no accidents in translation.

Mexico Sales Made Easy also ensures that you are kept up to date with any changes in laws or import regulations. In fact, with our finger so firmly on the pulse of importation law and customs regulations, we often have advance knowledge of such changes. This means we can be proactive in our approach to your requirements for your exports and sales into Mexico.

We Take the Strain: You have the Profit without the Pain

At *Mexico Sales Made Easy* we take the strain out of the export/ import process. Our decades of experience, good relations with customs officials and regulators, and our bilingual staff mean you have the Mexperts on your side. Paperwork is handled by fully trained representatives, relinquishing the expensive administrative process from your overworked export, sales, and accounts departments.

Your goods will reach your customer with less fuss and fewer delays. Your cash flow will benefit, your profitability will improve, and repeat orders will grow. Your reputation as an efficient exporter will grow. It will precede you as new customers seek you out. And we'll help you find those customers, too. Our reputation among Mexican importers is unrivalled, just as it is among U.S. exporters to Mexico. With the guarantee of fast, efficient, and hassle free importation on your side, your business will become the one with which Mexican importers want to conduct business.

Finally…

I'm so confident in Mexico as a place to sell to, and of **MSME**'s ability to help you with increasing your business, and profits that I've put everything you need to know and do in order to begin exporting and selling your products to Mexico in this book. When I told a few colleagues in the business that I was planning to write this book, they stared back in horror. Their reaction was, like, 'You're going to tell your customers *everything*?'

And that, perhaps, is the whole point. That's how **MSME** works. We work with you, our customer, keeping you fully informed of every step we take, and why we're taking it. Your business is selling. Our business is getting you and your product to the place where you can sell: Mexico.

Watch our video at: **http://www.mexicosalesmadeeasy.com**

Please feel free to visit **MSME**'s website, **www.mexicosalesmadeeasy.com**, and find out more about the business, and how we can help you with your exports to Mexico, and ask any questions you may have.

Regards

Sandro Piancone

Chapter 1

MEXICO – THE ECONOMY OF OPPORTUNITY

Facts You Need to Know About Mexico

Not too many people outside of Mexico or trade experts like ***MSME*** realize just how large the Mexican economy is, or how fast it is developing in world importance. In fact, if asked to name the G20, the likelihood is that Mexico would come well down on many U.S.-based business people's list, if, indeed, it appeared at all.

Get your monthly Mexpert Report FREE! Go to.....
www.mexicosalesmadeeasy.com

But with an economy measured in trillions of dollars, Mexico happens to be the world's 12th largest. It's a great export market for American companies with plenty of room for growth. Cross border trade between the U.S. and Mexico reached around $500 billion in 2011, and is still growing. This is not surprising, as Mexico not only has a large population – a 115 million residents it is the largest Hispanic country by numbers in the world – but a young and vibrant workforce.

The median age in Mexico is 27½, young compared to the United States or Canada, but just around the age that financial management begins to turn to real consumer spending. Half of Mexico's inhabitants, or 50 million people, are considered to be middle class, and only 7% are over 65 years old (though life expectancy is 77). It's easy to see that a major portion of the population is in the home growing and expenditure increasing mode of life.

And the good news doesn't stop there. The Mexican government is putting in place programs aimed at catapulting the nation to become one of the world's best-educated countries. Children and young adults are being encouraged to stay in education longer and the number of graduates these policies are producing continues to rise.

Based in stereotypes of the past, many people think of Mexico as a largely agricultural, pseudo-third world country, but that couldn't be further from the truth. It has a rapidly growing consumer base, and a social system that is encouraging an explosion in education, which has already led to an 86% literacy rate among teens. Mexico's economy is diverse and rapidly growing.

For example, Mexico's industrial base accounts for 34% of its economy, whereas agriculture is only 4%. The services sector in Mexico supplies the remainder of its national domestic product, more than half, a percentage that is likely to continue to expand. All of these facts are reasons for American exporters to be bullish about the prospects for business with Mexico, but the good news still doesn't stop there.

A Rapidly Growing Economy

Mexico was hit hard by the financial crisis of 2008, and saw the size of its economy shrink by a massive 6.2% in 2009 as a result. But the government took sizeable and swift measures, and has managed the economy well since. Consequently the bounce-back has been excellent.

In 2010, GDP grew by 5.4%, and this was followed by a further upturn of 3.8% in its economy in 2011. Now Mexico is well ahead of the economic downturn and continues to grow.

Today's circumstance includes a global economy experiencing the risk of another meltdown. The United States, Mexico's main trading partner, continues to suffer a sluggish rate of growth. The wisdom of the past would be that the Mexican economy would itself be slowing under such circumstances, but, in fact, the opposite is true.

The International Monetary Fund (IMF) has forecast that Mexican economic growth will hit 3.9% this year, and then dip only marginally to 3.6% in 2014. For a country that is second only to Canada in terms of

U.S. exports size, this is great news for all current and potential exporting U.S. companies.

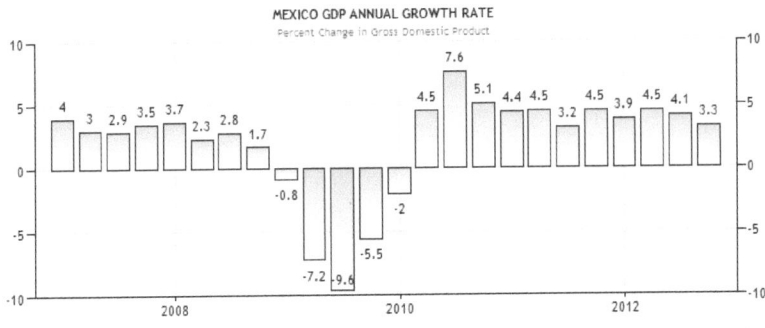

Mexico has plenty of room to continue this level of economic growth for years to come. We've already seen the potential for growth in its population and commitment to better education, but the policies and economic management of its government shouldn't be underestimated. It spent heavily to turn around the economy from the dark days of 2009, and yet its budget deficit is only 2.5% of its GDP. Mexico's net public debt is just 35.4% of GDP. Compare these numbers to the United States' budget deficit of around 8.25% of GDP and net debt of over 70% of GDP.

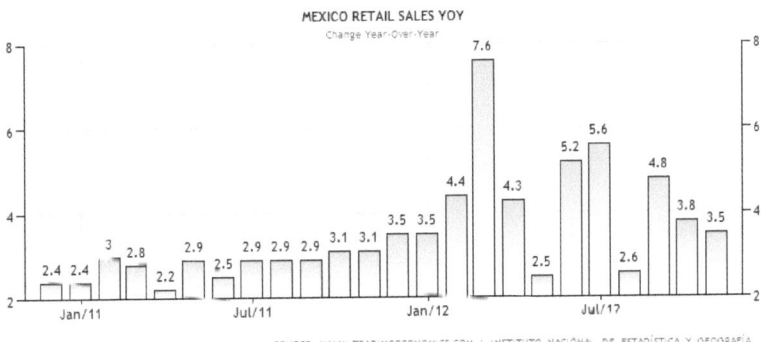

With an unemployment rate of just 5.2%, a diverse economy leaning heavily toward the service sector and a young population whose consumer mentality is growing along with its rising level of education;

it's easy to see that Mexico is an excellent market for exports from the United States for many years.

All of these facts are great news for those companies looking to export to Mexico, as is the dollar size of us/ Mexico cross border trade. Each day, approximately $1.25 billion of goods and services crosses between the two neighbors. The country is considered so important to the fortunes of American business that us-based businesses have invested over $145 billion in Mexico since 2000.

If you're not yet convinced of the opportunity that Mexico represents for your business, then perhaps we should compare it to another popular export destination. This country is not only in vogue, but considered by many to be the savior of American exporters.

China or Mexico: the Choice is Yours

You would not believe the number of CEOs or Vice Presidents of international corporations that I meet who are so excited about selling to China or India. They are happy to talk about the long grueling airplane trips, the choice of foods, speaking the language, etc. Then, I ask if their company is selling to Mexico. Most of them are not. I explain to them the advantages of close proximity, say that most deliveries can be made within a day, and most sales trips (depending where they are located) can be done within one day and they can still be home for dinner with their family. In fact, this is why the book is named "Discover The Secret Treasure Map to Selling Your Products in Mexico and Still be Home in Time for Dinner."

China is the world's second largest economy, having eclipsed Japan in 2010, and as it has been moving toward a more capitalist and consumer driven society, during its rapid period of growth. But the International Monetary Fund (IMF) predicts a rapid slowdown in its rate of growth over the coming years, and this will affect the opportunities for imports and trade.

While discussing China's imports – remembering that what really interests us are U.S. exports into China – it's worth noting the size of the market for U.S. companies. And here we're not considering the size of the population, but the actual real cash market. The reasons for examining it this way will become clear over the next couple of paragraphs. Much like other areas where publicity overtakes reality, the facts show that Mexico is a more lucrative market than China for us-based exporters.

In the first half of 2012, U.S. companies exported $52.8 billion of goods and services to China. Compare this number to the $106.5 billion of exports to Mexico.

Perhaps revisiting Mexico's economic make-up will help explain further the advantage of targeting Mexico rather than China.

Unlike China, Mexico's economy is already oriented toward the service sector. Though industry is a large contributor to GDP, and a large employer, increasingly Mexico is reliant on imported finished goods. The main exports to Mexico from the U.S. include mechanical machinery, electronic and electrical equipment, motor parts, fuels and oils, and plastics. Add into this mix consumer products and foodstuffs, and you begin to get some idea of the importance that Mexico places upon its business links and imports from the United States.

China remains a mainly industrial nation. It buys raw materials and then produces goods to sell domestically and for the export market. The Chinese may be looking to ignite the power of their consumers, but this will be for the benefit of its own industries and not for rapid growth of its import market. To put this in perspective, in 2011 China imported $129 billion of U.S. goods and services, while trade the other way totaled $411 billion.

But it's not just this systemic difference in economies that makes Mexico a more attractive proposition for companies that want to increase profits through exports. Geographically, Mexico is a far more affordable, easier target for U.S. exporters.

Mexico: a Single Border

Mexico and the United States share a common 2,000 mile border. They also share policing, transportation, environmental, and telecommunications responsibilities and duties. In 2010, Presidents Obama and Calderon created the Steering Committee for 21st Century Border Management, and there are initiatives between the two countries to promote trade. The major initiative is one whose name nearly everyone knows: the North American Free Trade Agreement (NAFTA).

As yet, there are few such agreements and pacts between the United States and China. And there is also a huge distance between the U.S. and China, over water.

It is far easier to transport goods to Mexico, by road or rail, and the trade agreements between the two countries have fostered even closer trade and cultural ties. Even though a large proportion of Mexico is Spanish speaking, the country's increasing education and a population of over 1 million United States' expats are changing these factors rapidly.

All in all, Mexico is a Great Place for Exports: but not Without Difficulties

On the positive side, Mexico has a strong and growing economy and great trade links with the United States. Its business and economic environment is more conducive to exporting by U.S. companies than China, and transportation links are in place and easy to negotiate. And yet companies in the United States often underestimate the opportunity just over the border, or consider it to be riddled with legal challenges that cause more cost and concern than end profit.

It's certainly true that there are administrative and legal issues to deal with in Mexico. Goods have to be properly classified, and valued for tax purposes. They have to be accompanied by complete NAFTA certificates (if NAFTA-originated), and exportation documentation can be more than a little problematic.

There are horror stories of even the largest U.S. companies falling foul of the Mexican importation process, and perhaps it is these stories that cause such pessimism among would-be exporters. And that's why using the right Mexperts is a must: someone who has the contacts, experience, and knowledge to ensure your exports clear customs and reach your customer promptly and without unnecessary cost to you.

Chapter 2

HISTORY IS ON YOUR SIDE

Ok, now a history lesson that they are probably not teaching in public schools or universities. It's not only the current economy that beckons the exporter. Just like an investor who wants to see the background and history behind an investment before he commits to it, so too does an exporting business. And in this regard, Mexico is better placed than almost any other target export market of the United States. Relationships have always been close – even if sometimes a little strained – between the two nations. But trade relations really began to take off in the early 1990's, with the introduction of NAFTA.

Get your monthly Mexpert Report FREE! Go to..... **www.mexicosalesmadeeasy.com**

NAFTA – A Brief History for the U.S. Exporter

In 1992, the North American Free Trade Agreement (NAFTA) was signed by the U.S. President, George H.W. Bush, the Mexican President, Salinas, and the Canadian Prime Minister, Brian Mulroney. It was ratified by all three countries legislatures in 1993, and came into force on January 1, 1994. NAFTA created the world's largest free trade zone. It has reduced the costs of trading, increased business investment, and increased global competitiveness for all three countries.

But it wasn't George H.W. Bush who first considered the importance of such a free trade zone, nor was it President Clinton, even though it is considered as one of his first successes. The NAFTA concept actually began with President Ronald Reagan, after Congress passed the Trade and Tariff Act in 1984. It was this Act that allowed the President to negotiate free trade agreements and cancelled the ability for Congress to change any of the negotiating points. Reagan could see how successful the European Union's continent-wide free trade agreement had become, and set himself the goal of creating a similar agreement on this side of the Atlantic.

His first step was the Canada-U.S. Free Trade Agreement in 1988, the success of which prompted President Bush to begin negotiations with Mexico to achieve a similar result. One of the main aims was to level the playing field between import and export tariffs. Prior to NAFTA, Mexican tariffs on U.S. imports were 250% higher than U.S. tariffs on Mexican imports, an imbalance problematic for businesses on both sides of the border. With these negotiations under way, Canada requested a trilateral agreement, and this led to the signing of NAFTA into the laws of all three countries.

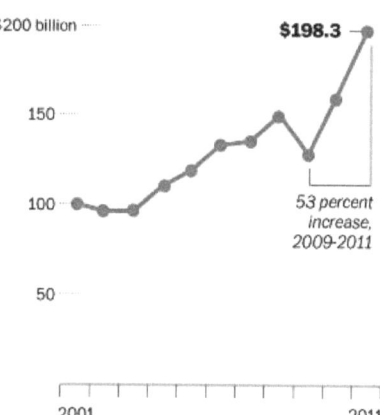

NAFTA Brings Advantages...

In less than less than 20 years, NAFTA has helped to see trade between the three member countries more than quintuple. In 1993, trade between the United States, Canada, and Mexico stood at a little under $300 million. By 2011 this had grown to over $1.7 trillion. U.S. exports within the Zone have grown to more than $450 billion, nearly half of which were to Mexico (see chart).

Low cost imports into the United States have also grown, to over $570 billion. Mexican oil exports to the United States benefited from the removal of tariffs, which has helped keep fuel prices in the United States lower than they would otherwise have been.

In addition, U.S. farm exports have been one of the main beneficiaries, with lower Mexican tariffs encouraging growth of more than 150% in this sector.

...but it Also has Some Disadvantages

Texas businessman Ross Perot, in 1992, said that he believed NAFTA would cost millions of Americans their jobs. In fact, he predicted that 5 million jobs would be lost to Mexico. Perot was incorrect. This has not been the case, though there has been some migration of companies, and therefore jobs, to Mexico's lower-cost labor base. NAFTA may also have helped keep wage inflation subdued in the United States. The threat of companies moving factories and production capacity to Mexico is seen by U.S.-based unions and workers as a very real one.

But the effect on jobs was not a one way street. Agriculture suffered in Mexico as cheap American imports from subsidized U.S. farming corporations hurt Mexican agricultural producers. With U.S. businesses setting up shop in Mexico, the Union movement and subsequently, Mexican labor laws, have been strengthened. Prior to NAFTA, Mexican workers had no labor rights or health protection. Now, more than a third of its workforce is in the 'maquiladora' program that gives such rights and protection.

NAFTA: Benefits Explodes Trade

The elimination of expensive tariffs has helped to reduce American inflation by decreasing the cost of imports from both neighboring countries, but particularly Mexico. This has helped usher in an unprecedented period of low interest rates, which has helped homebuyers with lower mortgage rates and also promoted retail businesses.

For businesses, agreements on rights for business investors has helped reduce the cost of trade, and this has been particularly good news for small businesses, where such costs have a far larger impact on margins.

Firms can now bid on cross border government contracts. In addition, one of the most important by-products of NAFTA is the protection of intellectual property rights across borders.

Politicians that have argued the detriments of NAFTA, and especially those that have called for its abolishment due to the effect on U.S. jobs, have largely been proved wrong. Hilary Clinton and Barack Obama have both attacked NAFTA. Clinton promised to strictly enforce all trade agreements and either amend or back out of NAFTA. Obama said it helped businesses at the expense of workers in the United States. Ron Paul, during the 2008 Presidential election campaign, said that he would abolish it, a position he maintained in his 2012 campaign. Going against the grain was Republican John McCain, who said he supported all free trade agreements as being ultimately good for the economy. So, which politician is right?

The truth, as usual, may be a bit of both. Certainly, some industries, such as automobile manufacturing, textiles, computers, and electrical equipment manufacturers have seen jobs lost to more competitive Mexican factory workers. This has also had an effect on wage inflation in the United States.

However, the flipside is that price inflation and interest rates have been lower than they would otherwise have been.

NAFTA has seen an explosion of trade between the three member countries, and exports from the U.S. to Mexico and Canada have ballooned, more than trebling during the course of NAFTA.

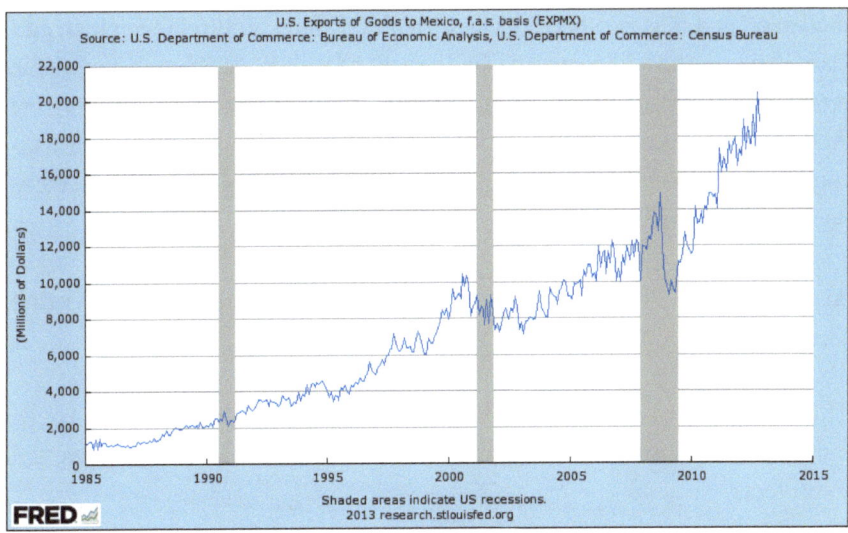

Despite dire warnings of politicians, one of the main beneficiaries in the U.S. from NAFTA has been the farming industry, which has seen exports to Mexico and Canada grow by well over 150%. U.S. farm exports to the rest of the world grew only 65% during the same period. Mexico is now the top destination for U.S. exported beef, soybean meal, corn sweeteners, apples, and beans, and the second-largest for corn, whole soybeans, and vegetable and seed oils.

The U.S. service industry has also seen a huge payday. With over 40% of the American economy operating in the service sector, being able to easily transport services to Mexico and Canada saw such exports grow from just $25 billion in 1993 to over $105 billion in 2007, before the financial crisis hit in 2008. The value of imports of services from Canada and Mexico is less than $40 billion.

It's not just cheaper tariffs that have helped U.S. inflation remain low. Imports of oil from Mexico have more than replaced imports of oil from Iran, and this in turn has helped America with cheaper fuel costs. And the elimination of food price tariffs has reduced food costs, too.

Americans have always invested abroad. But since NAFTA, Canadian and Mexican investment in U.S. business, negligible in the past, has increased at a massive pace. In fact, by 2009 (latest figures) Mexican and Canadian direct investment had reached over $235 billion. This represents investment into manufacturing, finance, and banking services. And that has been tremendous news for American business, which uses foreign investment money to grow and then export goods and services back to the investing country.

A Story of Politicians with Good Intentions: Unintended Consequences.

This is a story of how U.S. politicians wanting to help truckers, instead hurt farmers, Christmas tree growers and the same truckers they wanted to protect.

As you will see as you get to know me, I have no problem bashing both political parties on both sides of the border. Here is a story that really will blow your mind about NAFTA.

NAFTA's main aim is to increase trade in the North American zone, between Canada, the United States, and Mexico. And it has really been successful, as we have already seen. But for the success to be permanent, then there has to be a freedom not just of trade, but movement of goods, too: in other words, a breaking down of all trade barriers.

So NAFTA requires that each country signing up to it gives foreign service-providers 'treatment no less favorable' than she gives her own nationals. You would think that this would mean Mexican and Canadian trucks could take product across the border and deliver to importers.

So, in the 90's, President Clinton signed agreements for Mexican trucks to cross the border and ply their import deliveries to the U.S.A. But the Teamsters weren't happy about this. They objected to the fact that Mexican truck drivers are paid about half of what U.S. drivers are paid. The Teamsters argued that Mexican trucking companies would be coming over in the thousands and taking American trucker's jobs. They said that Mexican trucks and truckers were unsafe. So they lobbied Congress. The Speaker of the House at the time, Newt Gingrich, even said he expected 150,000 Mexican trucks to cross the border as soon as the restrictions were lifted.

The wheels in Washington move slowly. Eventually, because of this lobbying, President Obama put a stop to all of Clinton's plans with regard to Mexican trucks: Mexican trucks were restricted in the U.S. on safety grounds. That was a few years ago, and it unleashed a fair amount of mayhem.

Mexico wasn't about to sit down and take this action on the chin. They fought back, slapping a whole raft of tariffs on U.S. imports. But the Mexican government didn't announce a lead in period, or a period of reflection and time for dialogue and discussion. They announced the new duties and taxes, and they came into effect within seven days of the announcement.

Now, at that time, and while all this was going on, one of our clients had just signed a contract to sell 40 trucks per month (1,600,000 pounds) of cheese to a company in Mexico. They had already shipped 36 trucks at a cost of $3500 per truck in freight (contracted with a U.S. trucking company). The freight company was hired to haul the cheese from Wisconsin to Mexico. When the last 4 trucks of cheese were on the road, the taxes came into force. With 25% tax suddenly imposed upon the product, the export to Mexico suddenly became worthless: the cheese was never going to sell.

There was nothing our client could do, but to sell the cheese in the U.S.A at a loss. Their orders to their suppliers were cancelled. Trucking contracts were cancelled. The company lost money, truckers found themselves without work, farmers and producers lost jobs. The very thing that the Teamsters said they were protecting, the situation that Obama created, cost U.S. jobs and profits. And that was just a tiny microcosm of what happened, with one exporter out of tens of thousands affected.

Fortunately common sense has eventually prevailed(coincidentally after the 2010 elections), and, after new agreements were signed last year, earlier this year Mexican trucks have been allowed to apply for licenses to cross the border. Newt Gingrich and the scaremongers couldn't have been more wrong about the consequences of such a move. According to releases, and as reported in *The Trucker*, only 9 trucks and 11 drivers have entered the program!

The **San Diego Union reported** in February, 2012, that meetings were taking place between officials from the U.S. and Mexico with the aim of encouraging more Mexican truckers into the pilot program. The problem? Canacar, the trade association that represents individual carriers in the Mexican trucking industry, has said that the lack of enthusiasm has been caused by more stringent requirements placed upon Mexican truckers than their U.S. counterparts.

The process to apply and then be accepted into the cross-border trucking program is "complicated, expensive and hasn't brought any benefit" according to Juan Carlos Munoz Marquez, Canacar's national president, and owner of Transportes Castor, one of Mexico's largest trucking companies.

The current situation comes at a time when there is a **chronic shortage of truckers in the U.S.A**. Because of this shortage, freight rates are rising; meaning the costs of goods for export are rising. Drivers' pay rates are rising rapidly, too. At least the Teamsters got that right, I suppose.

Chapter 3

YOUR BUSINESS IS YOUR TRADEMARK

Have you already trademarked your brand in Mexico? If not, it could already be too late.

One of our Titanium clients, Queso Nery's, which produces a well-known cheese brand in Mexico, had been having a good amount of success with exporting its American and Mexican-style cheeses into Mexico. I'd personally helped the company reach out to Mexico-based distributors and importers, and its good name and brand presence had started to spread well.

Get your monthly Mexpert Report FREE! Go to….. **www.mexicosalesmadeeasy.com**

Then something strange started to happen. Queso Nery's sales, which had been growing well week-to-week and month-to-month, started to reverse. The company hadn't changed tack, and was still spending money on promotion and advertising, but those sales that had begun to explode had suddenly taken a turn for the worse.

The client couldn't understand what was happening, and neither could we, until we found some copycat products on Mexican shop shelves. Our client was having his trademark copied and traded under by a Mexican rival. The client, understandably, was furious. Fortunately, it had properly trademarked its company and products, both in Mexico and the United States. A lot of companies don't realize that their trademark needs to be separately registered in Mexico. It's not good enough just having the trademark in the United States, because Mexico has its own trademark laws.

But Mexican trademark laws also give a company the right to fight back, and that's what we did for the client. We fought, hard. Much the same as in the United States, defending a trademark in Mexico is a pretty complex process, with plenty of form filling to be done, but we worked with our client and pushed the case through the Institute de la Propiedad Industrial (IMPI), aka the Mexican Institute of Industrial Property, the PRG and the U.S. Federal government. *Queso Nery's* received a cease and desist order against the Queso Nery's copycat, and our client turned its business round to growth again.

If Queso Nery's hadn't had their trademark registered properly in the first place, there would have been precious little that we, or they, could have done. And the last thing any business wants is anyone copying their trademark and selling on the back of their hard-earned quality and good name.

Just imagine how bad it could have been for Queso Nery's. All that money spent entering a new market and building product presence, to see a great position usurped? Our client had done the right thing by registering its trademark, and then we were able to help quickly when trademark infringement happened. The Queso Nery's experience is why one of the first things I recommend to clients is to register their trademarks in Mexico.

What is a trademark?

In the U.S. as well as in Mexico, a trademark shows the source of the goods, and allows the consumer to distinguish between one manufacturer and another. It's a mark of the quality of a business and its product. It helps a customer quickly identify other goods made by the same manufacturer, and then the reputation associated with that trademark promotes sales of those other goods. A trademark can tell current and prospective customers all about the history, quality, and even the origin of a product.

A trademark is also about the goodwill that a company and its products have built up. This directly affects the price at which a company can sell its products. Goodwill is impossible to separate from the reputation of a company. We all know that a good reputation takes years to build, but minutes to destroy.

More than just lost sales, when a product is sold by the use of a copied trademark – so called parallel selling – the expectations that have been built up within the consumer can be destroyed. Quality and value are likely to be missing in such products. Here are just a few of the factors of customer satisfaction that may be affected:

- No after sales service
- No guarantees honored
- Packaging and instructions in poor language
- Poor instructions
- Reusability and recyclability inaccuracies on packaging
- Health information or nutritional value miss-advice

Not only will the good name of the company be affected, but also its product sales, both now and in the future. As we have already covered, I want to remind you again: just because a trademark is registered and protected in the United States, it is not also protected in Mexico by the same process. Some of the largest companies have fallen foul of this misconception, as I will show you in a short while.

Trademarks in Mexico – The Law

Mexico is not part of the Madrid Protocol, which allows simultaneous registration of trademarks in several countries. Separate registration has to be made in Mexico, and trademark registration in Mexico can take months. In Mexico, after it is registered, the trademark remains registered for a period of ten years and is automatically renewable.

A trademark can be practically anything applicable to a corporation's products, including words, symbols, logos, and designs, as well as trade names, and three dimensional goods that are distinctive of a trademarks – such as a perfume bottle, or container. Of course, a trademark could include combinations of all of these.

The trademark needs to be registered with the Mexican Trademark Authority, IMPI. Once this is complete, it is best to arrange protection with the Mexican Customs Border Authority. This action will stop counterfeit goods at the border, protecting your business is Mexico and the U.S. *MSME* can arrange this protection for you.

Make sure your Apple isn't poisoned

In early November 2012, Apple, Inc. lost a trademark battle in Mexico. The case had started in 2009, and involves its U.S. and (almost) worldwide trademark, iPhone. You see, unbeknownst to Apple, when it began to market its key product in Mexico in 2007, there was already a company called iFone trading in the country.

The Mexican telecoms company, iFone, had been trading under its name for four years before Apple started to market its iPhone product in Mexico. In 2009, iFone filed a lawsuit claiming trademark infringement against the U.S. corporate giant, saying that the similar names caused confusion to its customers and consumers in Mexico.

Now it would appear that Apple will need to compensate iFone for the use of the iPhone name in Mexico.

What this story demonstrates is the strength of the copyright law in Mexico: if a company's trademark is registered in Mexico, no matter how large a company comes along with its own product, the original will be protected by law.

Properly registering your trademark in Mexico will mean you can take a bite of the business apple without fear of it being poisoned against you.

The IMPI

The IMPI is the public agency that manages all industrial trademarks in Mexico, and as such, application for trademark registration has to be made to it.

For any trademark applicant who resides outside of Mexico, a power of attorney must be given to handle the application for trademark registration and protection. The POA must be signed in the presence of two witnesses, and it must also state that the person signing on behalf of the company wanting to apply for trademark registration has the authority to do so.

If the applicant is not identical to the holder of the internationally recognized trademark supporting the application, then papers of assignment of the trademark to the applicant will also need to be furnished with the application forms.

Payment of all fees must be made with the application, and these payments cover the filing fee, and trademark examination fees. This fee has to be paid in Mexican pesos and be submitted with his application.

This may sound a complex and drawn out process (it can take up to 12 months to move from application to registration). It may be that the need to complete application forms in Spanish fills you with dread. But it's certain that your business will benefit from trademark protection, and suffer without it. It's the first thing you must do before selling in Mexico.

Resources:
Here are the links to the Mexican Institute of Industrial Property (Instituto Mexicano de Propiedad Industrial, or IMPI) and Mexican Government Trademark Search Engine:

Mexico Patent and Trademark Office (IMPI)
http://www.impi.gob.mx/

Mexican Government Search Engine for Trademarks
http://marcanet.impi.gob.mx/marcanet/controler/home

Of course, doing business in Mexico and accessing a market with tens of millions of potential customers doesn't end with trademark registration. Your products also have to be labeled correctly, and if they're not... let's see what happened to Wal-Mart when its labels failed to meet Mexican legal requirements.

Chapter 4

TRADEMARKS IDENTIFY, LABELS EXPLAIN

In 2007/8, the world's largest retailer, Wal-Mart, was well and truly riding the wave of the Mexican retail revolution promoted by NAFTA. It was opening new stores almost on a weekly basis, and sales were rocketing. Everything was rosy in the Wal-Mart garden, and it was exporting huge amounts of stock across the border. This was, perhaps, the perfect example of how NAFTA could provide success for all: an American retailer, with store locations in Mexico employing Mexican people and selling goods made by American suppliers and exported from the United States to Mexico. Wal-Mart's story at this time showed a trade zone working in perfect harmony.

Get your monthly Mexpert Report FREE! Go to….. www.mexicosalesmadeeasy.com

But trouble was brewing.

Wal-Mart failed to change many of its labels to display product information in Spanish. And the Spanish authorities didn't like that. Wal-Mart claimed that it was a computer glitch that had caused the mistake, and then blamed human error. Whatever the problem was, the Mexican authorities didn't take kindly to Wal-Mart's protestations. They told Wal-Mart to change its labels. And then they shut down the Mexico City store until Wal-Mart complied with the order.

According to the Fortune Global 500 list, Wal-Mart is the world's third largest public corporation, employing over 2 million people in more than 8500 stores around the globe. And yet a company of this size and stature made a basic error: it failed to act on legal requirements and advice, or, perhaps, it just didn't realize what the rules of exportation were.

Mexican labeling rules can be quite complex and hidden away within the wording of NOM-51, the labeling law for foods and beverages in Mexico.

Welcome to Mexico NOMs, a law That Makes Everything Clearer!

The requirements for labeling products in preparation for export to Mexico can be very complex, particularly for food products and nutritional supplements. Fortunately, all the details are contained within the appropriate laws in Mexico, including NOM-51. However, as with many laws, NOM-51 is subject to ad hoc amendments that are designed to keep the law up-to-date with modern practice. Further, the law and amendments are written in Spanish.

Here are some basics regarding NOM-51 and other NOMS for other types of products. At a minimum, product labels must be in Spanish. These labels must be on the product when they are imported into Mexico, and if they aren't then, the import will be stopped at the border and held. There may be exemptions, but these are few and far between, and have to be arranged months in advance with labels provided for affixing within Mexico.

Typically, products must be labeled with the following information:

- Product name
- Quantity or amount
- Name, registration number and address of the producer
- Name, registration number and address of the importer
- Country of origin (and there are special rules here)
- Relevant warnings
- Instructions, or reference to an instruction manual, if appropriate

There are laws that cover labeling requirements for textiles, pre-packaged foods and non-alcoholic beverages, and further laws to cover other consumer products not covered by other laws!

Certain goods, such as silver-plated products, leather goods and clothing have one set of labeling rules, while other textiles and apparel have to comply with a separate set of requirements.

Under NOM51, food and non-alcoholic beverages also have to include:

- Expiration date
- Storage instructions
- Preparation and use instructions

Again, all of this must be in Spanish.

Common mistakes are made time and again

Wal-Mart's experience was a big case at the time, and served to highlight the problems of non-translated labeling. Yet still many exports from the United States to Mexico are held up at the border, or even confiscated, never to be seen again, because labeling is in English.

Many companies also believe that a straight translation on current U.S. product labeling, from English to Spanish, will suffice. But this is not the case, as there are additional items of information needed on product labels to comply with not just import labeling requirements but general labeling requirements.

Common mistakes are often made because exporters try to cut corners, using the in-house expertise of employees who only work part-time on an area of competence that requires full- time maintenance. As Wal-Mart discovered, a few dollars saved on the U.S. side of the border can cost millions in Mexico.

Resources:

NOM 51 Requirements
http://dof.gob.mx/nota_detalle.php?codigo=5137518&fecha=05/04/2010

Now you have your trademark registered and protected, and your products are labeled correctly for the Mexican market, you can start exporting, right? Well, you're not quite there yet. Before your products leave on their way to the importer, you need to make sure that you, or your customers in Mexico, won't be paying unnecessary taxes. Avoiding these unnecessary expenditures means you need to understand product classification.

Chapter 5

CLASSIFY YOUR PRODUCT – IT'S YOUR DUTY

Know Your HS Number

This story goes back to when I first started exporting to Mexico. It's a big lesson that I teach everyone: you need to know your HS number, because no one else cares. I began my career as an export manager for my family's nationwide pizza distribution company, Roma Food (www.romafood.com). My job was to travel around Mexico and convince distributors to buy our many products including flour to make pizza. At the time, we sold to Mexico, not in Mexico. So our delivery was to the border, and the importer/distributor took care of everything else.

After a while we had several distributors as customers around Mexico, using different import agencies to manage the trade of goods between U.S. and the importers. Talking to one of my distributors, I discovered that he had been paying a 5% import duty on the flour for many years. While speaking to my other distributors, I found out they were not paying the 5% duty on the flour.

Get your monthly Mexpert Report FREE! Go to….. www.mexicosalesmadeeasy.com

Needless to say, my distributor was more than a little upset when he was told that the flour he had been buying from us should have no duty applied to it. For years it had been paying its 5%, meaning its margins were lower and costs higher, when it should have paid nothing. It may even have been that sales had been lost because of a lack of competitiveness in pricing. The cost to the distributor amounted to thousands of dollars. The reason was that his import agency misclassified the flour product. The agency classified it as all-purpose flour, when in fact it was special flour for pizza with certain characteristics. I learned the lesson then, that most agencies are lazy and do not care about which HS classification they assign, because it is not their money. You need to know your HS Classification number to avoid the fate of paying extra and unnecessary taxes and duties.

What are HS Classification Codes?

Product classification codes are used to determine the rate and amount of duties and taxes that have to be paid on imported goods. The Harmonized Commodity Description and Coding System (HS) is recognized around the world as a standardized system of names and numbers for classifying traded products. It has been developed and is maintained by the World Customs Organization (WCO).

The WCO sets these numbers, and countries are obliged to use them. However, though tariff schedules are based upon HS, countries will set their own rates of duties upon these categories.

The system allows exporting and importing nations to keep track of trade, and monitor and collect taxes. The tax collecting part of the process is undertaken by customs authorities, and higher duties are levied on the goods that are in competition with internal manufacturers in each country that produce the same or similar goods. If there is no competitive product made within a country's borders, then duties can't be levied.

Some goods won't need an import permit, while others will. The classification process is part of the overall framework that enables the correct identification of those goods that require a permit as against those that don't. Incorrect classification could mean unnecessary time and effort applying for import permits, as well as the financial implications of wrongly taxed goods.

Importing products to Mexico is only viable if the cost of doing so is not so outside the realms of competitiveness. In general, retail taxes are levied on all goods, but import duties are there to protect domestic business. The idea behind this is that import duties will bring the cost of imported goods into line with domestic goods and negate competitive advantage on price only.

Goods that are misclassified could have import duties applied that are above the legal requirement. Not only will this harm price competitiveness, but none of the charges that are incurred can be reclaimed later when the mistake is discovered.
Another concern regarding the HS number is a match between importation and exportation documentation. For goods to clear border customs authorities, importation and exportation documentation must match, including the HS number. Mismatching will cause goods to be stuck at the border, incurring further costs and delays on their way to point of sale.

Classification of goods is a complicated process, and requires attention to detail. For example, the simple task of classifying an oven for export/import needs confirmation of the type of oven it is – gas, electric, etc. – as well as the use of the oven – domestic or industrial. In other words, goods for import to Mexico have to be classified as to their form and their function.

NAFTA and HS

U.S. products either have minimal duties or are exempted from duties altogether when imported into Mexico. However, the rules of origin are stringent. This ensures that the goods are indeed produced in the United States, and not manufactured elsewhere before final export to Mexico.

Under NAFTA, a Certificate of Origin must be signed by the exporter. An exporter who is not a producer of goods can request the producer to provide the certificate for him, but the obligation to do so remains with the exporter.

The exporter must pass the Certificate of Origin to the importer, and this will then be presented to Customs in order to qualify for preferential rates of importation duties. Where the product doesn't qualify for NAFTA tariff preferences, then the Certificate must not be completed as the import may qualify for other preferential treatment under the Most Favored Nation (MFN) tariff rates.

The NAFTA rules of origin are organized to coincide with the HS, and the first step to take to assess qualification for preferential importation duties is to determine the correct HS number.

After this has been determined, then the appropriate tariff can be assessed. If the MFN rate is zero, then no NAFTA certificate is required. If the MFN rate is not zero, then the HS number should be used to locate the applicable rule of origin under NAFTA, and determination of the NAFTA rate can be made.

The Certificate of Origin

The Certificate of Origin requires the names and addresses of exporters, producers, and importers, as well as a full description of goods, relevant HS numbers, costs, and declaration of origin, and must be filled in if the goods being exported, or likely to be exported during a 'blanket period' of up to one year, exceeds $1000 in value.

Producer Name

The first and last name of the producer of the goods must be provided, and included with the company name of the producer (if applicable).

Tariff Code

The Tariff Code is the product specific HS number, and will be between 6 and 10 digits.

Exporter/ Shipper of Goods

It has to be stipulated if the shipper is the producer. If not, then if the goods qualify as originating goods, the level of reliance on the producer that the goods qualify as originating goods, or the completed and signed Certificate of Origin must be provided to the exporter by the producer.

Avoid Common Mistakes

Even experienced exporters and importers, including multi-national companies, get their HS codes wrong and incorrectly complete Certificates of Origin. Sometimes, as in the case of the pizza importer/distributor highlighted earlier, misclassified goods manage to cross the border for years. This never occurs when goods are misclassified with a lower than required tariff, only when the tariff is higher than it should be.

Misclassification will cost time, goodwill, and, perhaps most importantly, money. It can mean products crossing the border becoming uncompetitive in your target market.

Resources:
The Census Bureau has a simple-to-use free tool at their website and a short instructional video that shows you how to find the exact 10 digit code you need. Here's the handy link:

Schedule B Search Engine:
https://uscensus.prod.3ceonline.com/

The Bottom Line

As you can probably see, I'm very passionate about doing business in Mexico. I think that there are plenty of great companies in the United States that are missing out on a great opportunity by ignoring the market just across the border. I've helped small companies get big by taking them to Mexico.

A growing market waits for you. The reason I wrote this book is so that you, too, can see the huge potential that is Mexico. I hope that I've helped you: hopefully you've learned a lot, and now have the tools to start out on the exciting journey to exporting your product to Mexico.

Of course, this book only deals with the beginning of your journey. Once you've started on your journey, then you'll also need to fully understand the intricacies of marketing and selling in Mexico, and how to reach out to prospective customers, importers, and distributors. And after you've done that, then the execution of your export strategy, delivering products and logistics.

CASE STUDIES

Here's a few of the companies that I have helped with their journey into trading with Mexico.

Nery's Logistics

Nery's Logistics is the largest Titanium client for *Mexico Sales Made Easy*.

We handle all of its trademark issues, NOM labeling requirements, and HS classifications for the many diverse products that the company imports and delivers. These products include pizza products, restaurant equipment, and now 5 Hour Energy Shots.

Nery's Logistics is one of the most respected and sought after foodservice logistics companies in Mexico, and it covers the whole country from 5 strategically placed warehouses. When you are ready to start exporting to Mexico, Nery's Logistics can handle all of your logistics needs.

For more information, visit **www.neryslogistics.com**

Queso Nery's

Another of my Titanium clients and MSME's first client.

Again, I have handled all of its trademarking requirements as well as prepared entry for new products and their HS classifications.

Queso Nery's are great to work with, and know all about introducing new and exciting products to Mexico. It is a great company to work with, and is always coming up with new and exciting products.

Check out its website **www.quesonerys.com.**

U.S. Tobacco De Mexico

It, too, is a Titanium member, but by far our hardest challenge which keeps us on our toes. It imports Grade A cigarettes from North Carolina into Mexico under several private label programs. We handle all trademarking issues, HS Classifications and permitting processes and NOM labeling on the cigarettes. And this is where the real challenge comes in and where *Mexico Sales Made Easy* excels far beyond other companies. Mexico now makes manufacturers put Pictograms on all cigarette packages. That's easy enough, but to make things more complex, Mexican law insists that these are changed every 3 months.

That's a hard job that we conduct for the client, keeping on top of changing legal requirements and making sure the exporter's products can still enter Mexico.

To learn more about their business visit their website **www.ustobaccodemexico.com**

About the Author: Sandro Piancone

Sandro is a serial entrepreneur. He started his first business at the age of ten, placing video games in retail outlets such as pizza shops, restaurants, bars, and cafes for a friend of his father. The late 1970's were a great time for people in the video gaming business, and Sandro was paid $50 for each placement he made: big money back then, especially for one so young in business. Somehow, Sandro spotted the top of the market, took his profits, and moved to a more lucrative hobby and business: collecting comic books.

But that was then. Having founded and built up several successful businesses since, he now describes himself as a 'recovering' CEO of a publicly traded foodservice company in Mexico. Sandro has introduced a number of U.S. brands to Mexico, and helped to build them to multi-million dollar brands: including Miller Beer, Thrifty Ice Cream, Roma Food, and Rockstar Energy Drinks. He sits on several corporate boards, advising on issues such as trademark and labeling requirements. He presently works with clients including Little Caesars Pizza, Queso Nery's, Nery's Logistics, and 5-hour Energy. Since 1998, he has generated well over $500 million dollars in sales and profits for his clients and partners, helping them export their products into Mexico.

He works long and hard to make sure that his clients, and their products, move to market as quickly and smoothly as possible with no problems and the highest profits.

You see, in his own businesses he's made all the mistakes that could possibly have been made in transitioning from the United States to Mexico. He's had product stopped at the Mexican border because the paperwork was fouled up. But only once. He's seen his product sales hit by unfair competition issues inside Mexico. But only once. Every time he's made a mistake, he's learned from it.

It's this experience, a dedication to great customer care, and an attitude of providing flawless execution of tasks that he not only brings to Mexico Sales Made Easy, but also instills in all his staff.

While not travelling throughout Mexico, Sandro lives in San Diego with his amazing wife K, and his 2 cute M&Ms. He enjoys collecting rare "signed first edition" books (both comic books and autobiographies.)

Get your monthly Mexpert Report FREE! Go to….. **www.mexicosalesmadeeasy.com**

His office is in San Diego, California. Should you wish to contact him directly about consulting, speaking, or just comment about the book please e-mail him at **spiancone@mexicosalesmadeeasy.com** or call his offices at (619) 616-2973.

How Would You Like To Make Sales Presentations to at Least 3 Of The Largest Supermarket Buyers in Mexico Without Having To Make A Single Call Or Setup A Single Meeting?

Come and join

The MEXICO CEO Tour 2014

Discover the Secret Treasure Map to selling your products in Mexico

March 10-14, 2014

Presented by

Hosted by

Sandro Piancone, Chief Mexpert Officer

Dear CEO, President, top executive or business owner looking to expand your business in Mexico!

This is your opportunity to get it **_all_** direct from the horse's mouth; the insider tour for <u>every</u> exporter trying to sell to Mexico, fully supported with facts and data and real live examples and case histories.

I am preparing **THE most complete and detailed and valuable multi-day Training on this business that has ever been presented.** And regardless of your experience level in exporting to Mexico, I guarantee this, in your judgment, to be worth, *really* worth hundreds of thousands of dollars or more to you and your business.

PLEASE REQUEST A COPY OF THE PREVIEW BRIEFING WITH COMPLETE DETAILS ABOUT THE MEXICO CEO TOUR FROM THE MEXICO SALES MADE EASY OFFICE <u>IMMEDIATELY.</u>

At this writing, fewer than 12 spots remain available in Tour with spots being taken daily. Whether you are an experienced export veteran OR someone getting started or looking in and contemplating a exporting to Mexico, you should get and consider this information and this opportunity.

TO REQUEST YOUR PREVIEW BRIEFING:
Go to <u>ceo.mexicosalesmadeeasy.com</u>

How to Reach Your Free Gifts?

FREE - Newsletter $99 value
www.mexicosalesmadeeasy.com/freenewsletter.html

FREE Trademark Search in Mexico $249
www.mexicosalesmadeeasy.com/trademark.html

FREE - Special Report -
3 Things you absolutely need to do before selling in Mexico

FREE - Special Report -
Top 5 Reasons your product will get stuck at the border

www.mexicosalesmadeeasy.com/report.html

www.ingramcontent.com/pod-product-compliance
Lightning Source LLC
Chambersburg PA
CBHW041109180526
45172CB00001B/169